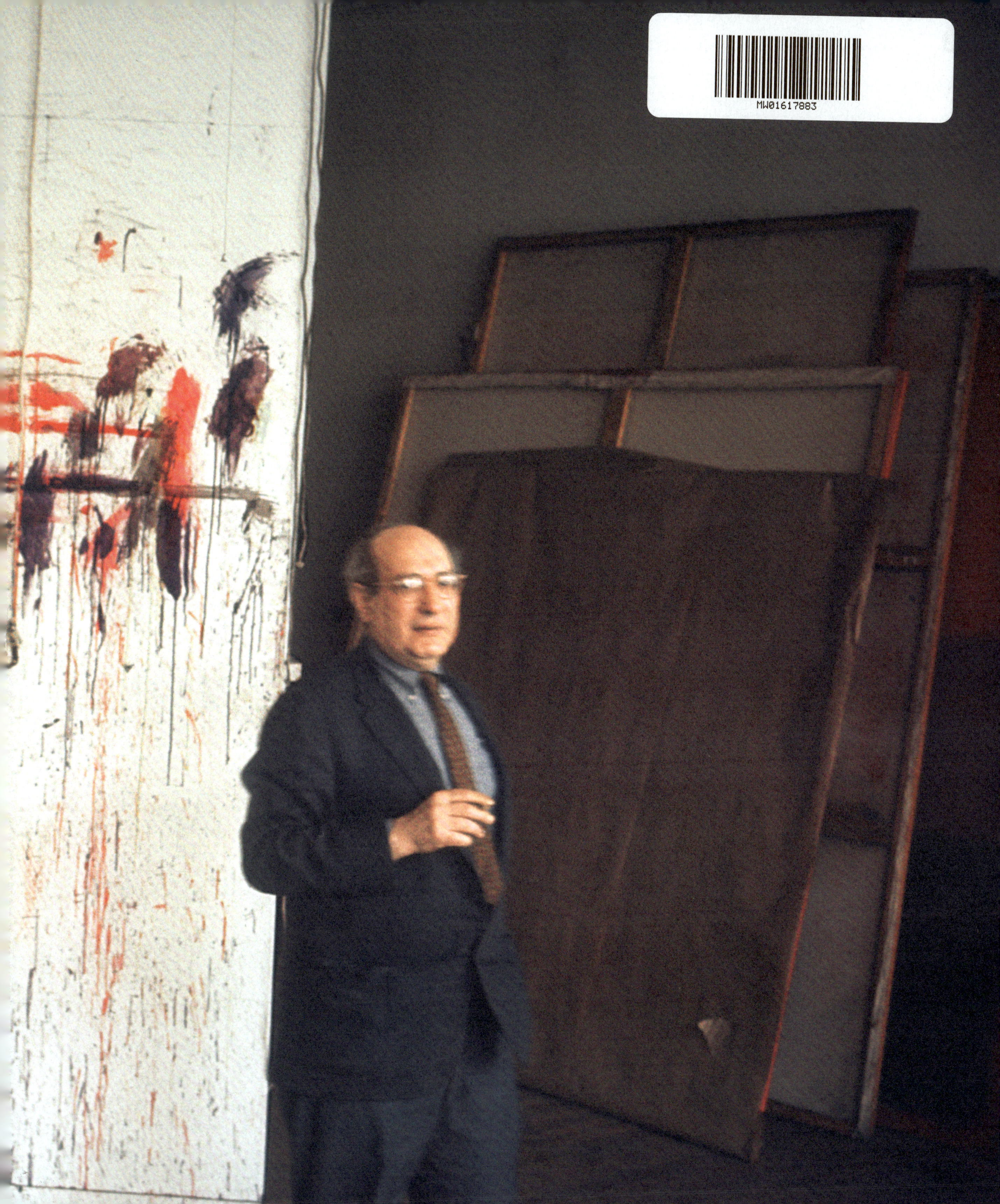

ROTHKO

ROTHKO

PACE

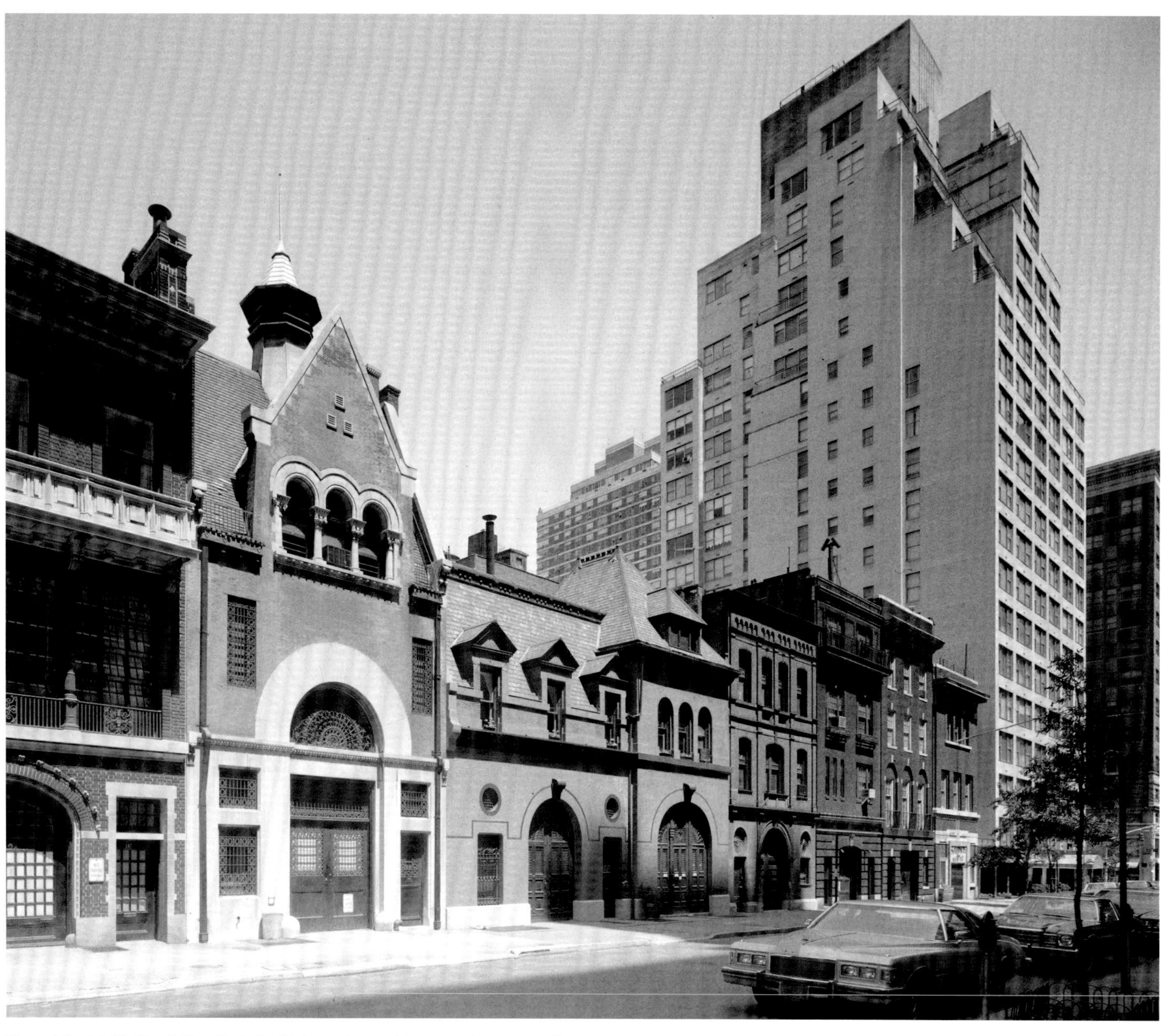

View of East 69th Street, New York. Rothko's studio, 157 East 69th Street, third from left

INTRODUCTION

1968

It's six o'clock and I'm on my way home from the gallery when I pass Mark Rothko's studio, which is just across the street from my apartment. I spontaneously ring the bell, as I have done so many times before. Mark answers the door and welcomes me in. It's always a thrill to see what new paintings might be there. Hanging on the wall is an enormous painting of dark blue and black soft rectangles floating on a deep burgundy field. I am in awe of its magnificence and I tell Mark that I'm knocked out by the painting. He laughs and tells me the following story.

Mark selected this particular painting for a collector who had been asking him for a work for some time. It was Mark's practice to select the work that he felt best suited the collector, or collection, into which it might fit. Disappointed by his choice, she rejected the painting. "Mr. Rothko," she said, "I want a happy painting, not a sad painting. A pink and red and orange and yellow painting, a joyous painting." "Pink, red, orange, and yellow," Rothko mused. "Aren't those the colors of an inferno?" She left without a painting and he didn't offer her any other work.

On several occasions, Mark spoke of the importance of tragedy and tragic themes as stimuli for the creation of profound beauty. Rothko considered tragedy a theme worthy of art. He cited Greek theater and the way in which it dealt with the depth of human emotions and universal truths. Although the colors, composition, and levels of intensity change, heroic themes permeate his paintings.

This exhibition presents the dark-value paintings that were produced throughout his career and they disprove the prevalent interpretation that the dark paintings function as an end game; the product of depression and impending doom. Mark didn't paint when he was depressed. Painting was a positive, exultant experience for him. His life's work was the expression of pure emotion and color was his medium.

Arne Glimcher

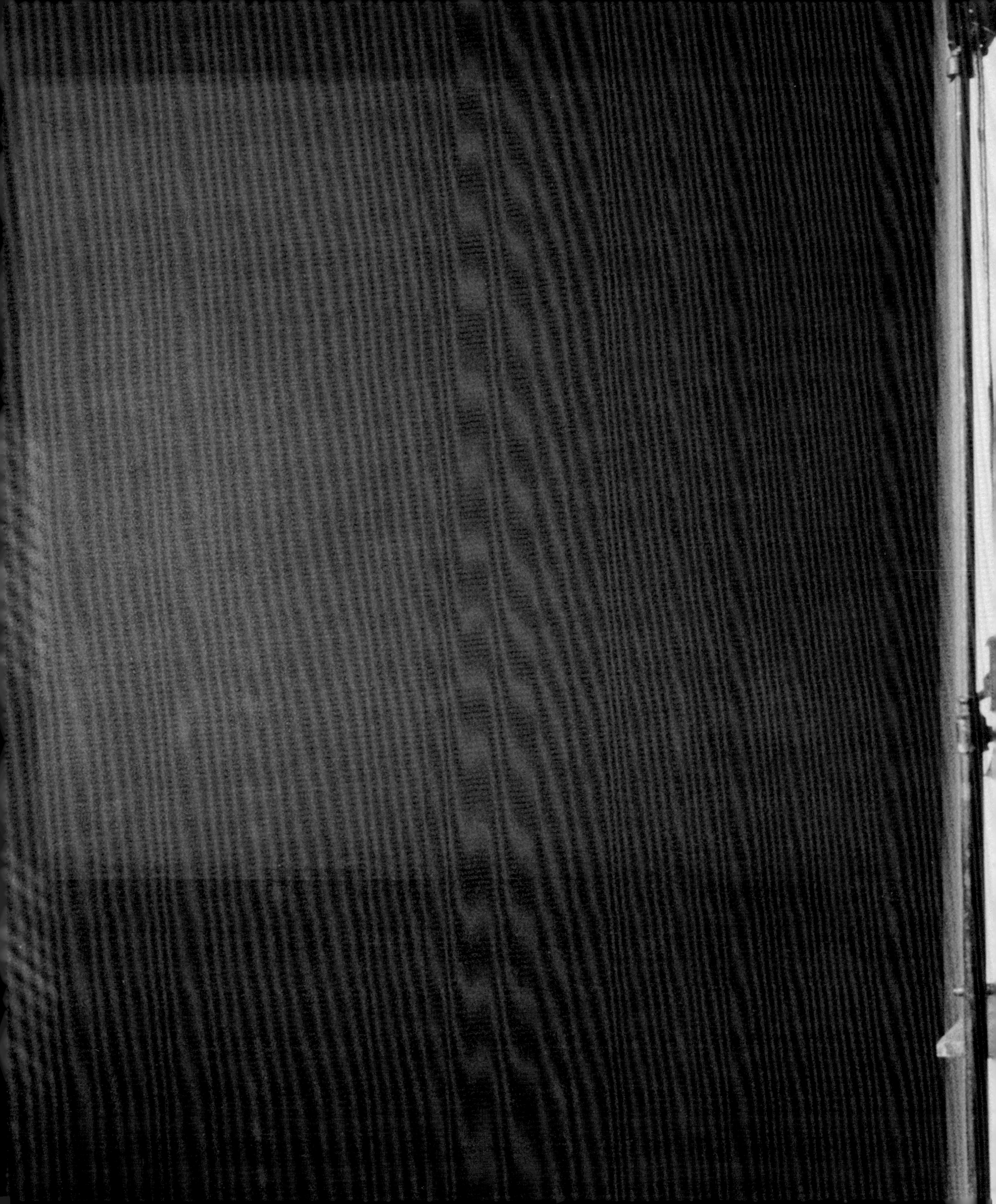

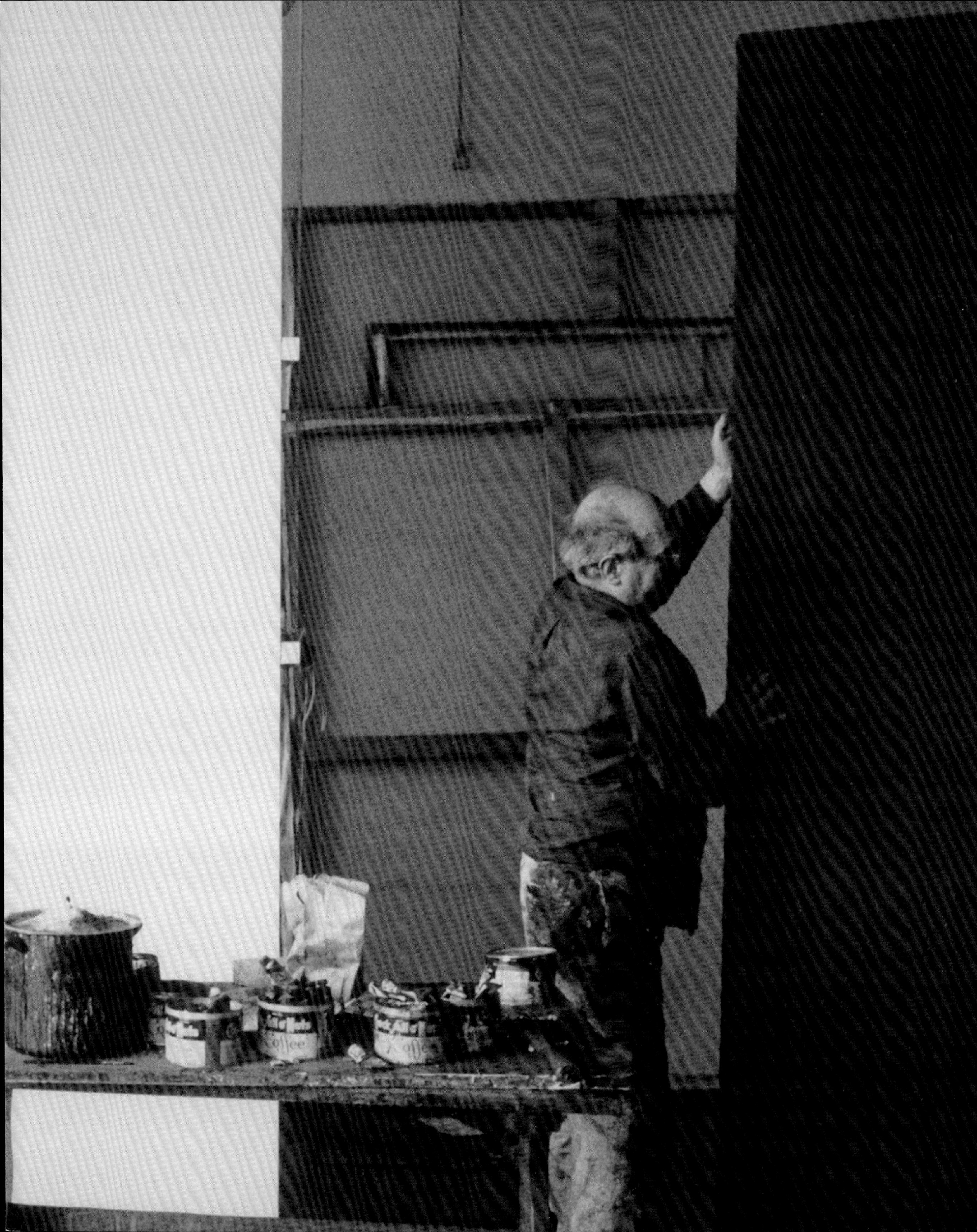
Coffee
Coffee

The recipe of a work of art—its ingredients—how to make it—the formula.

1. There must be a clear preoccupation with death—intimations of mortality. . . Tragic art, romantic art, etc., deals with the knowledge of death.
2. Sensuality. Our basis of being concrete about the world. It is a lustful relationship to things that exist.
3. Tension. Either conflict or curbed desire.
4. Irony. This is a modern ingredient—the self-effacement and examination by which a man for an instant can go on to something else.
5. Wit and play. . .for the human element.
6. The ephemeral and chance. . .for the human element.
7. Hope. 10% to make the tragic concept more endurable.

I measure these ingredients very carefully when I paint a picture. It is always the form that follows these elements and the picture results from the proportions of these elements.

—Mark Rothko

UNTITLED 1955 oil on canvas 81 ½ x 59 ⅝"

Collection of Kate Rothko Prizel

. . . but 1957 is also the year that my father marked as the year his "dark pictures" began. In fact, the assertion is rather misleading: there are wonderfully rich dark paintings from the early 1950s as well as brilliant ones after 1957. While it is true that there is general darkening of the palette in the last thirteen years of my father's career, the changes in form are at least equally responsible for the more meditative mood of the later works.

—Christopher Rothko

BLACK IN DEEP RED 1957 oil on canvas 69 3/8 x 53 3/4"

Private collection, Santa Monica, California

NO. 37 / NO. 19 (SLATE BLUE AND BROWN ON PLUM) 1958 oil on canvas 95 ¼ x 86 ¼"

The Museum of Modern Art, New York. Given anonymously

Color, the expressive medium most associated with Rothko, was of course a central player in his quest to produce what is essentially installation art. The Seagram commission pushed Rothko to create a new color scheme that was cohesive yet varied enough to stimulate the viewer, an overall effect that maintained areas of local interest. With the known proportions of an exclusively Rothko room, he could harness color and form to create an experiential unity whose power lay in its simplicity and its understated, unwavering presence.

Rothko had begun darkening his palette in 1957, the year before he began the Seagram series, but the rich burgundies that would become his hallmark began in earnest with the murals. Saturated and just past ripe, this color would form the background for all three series he painted. Sometimes veering more toward wood tones, occasionally with a hint of purple, it is the very flesh of these works. As with his forms, Rothko found a robustly physical color; deeply sensual, never flamboyant.

—Christopher Rothko

◂ **MURAL, SECTION 6 (UNTITLED) [SEAGRAM MURAL]** 1959 oil on canvas 6 x 15'

Collection of Kate Rothko Prizel and Christopher Rothko

UNTITLED 1960 oil on canvas 79 1/2 x 69 1/4"

Virginia Museum of Fine Arts, Richmond. Gift of Sydney and Frances Lewis

NO. 22 (UNTITLED) 1961 oil, acrylic and mixed media on canvas 79 ½ x 69 ½"

Albright-Knox Art Gallery, Buffalo, New York; Gift of The Mark Rothko Foundation, Inc., 1985

UNTITLED (RUST, BLACKS ON PLUM) 1962 oil on canvas 60 x 57"

Private collection

I'm interested only in expressing basic human emotions—tragedy, ecstasy, doom, and so on—and the fact that lots of people break down and cry when confronted with my pictures shows that I *communicate* those basic human emotions.

—Mark Rothko

UNTITLED (DARK GRAY ON MAROON) 1963 oil, acrylic and mixed media on canvas 11' 2 ½" x 6' ⅛"

National Gallery of Art, Washington, D.C. Gift of The Mark Rothko Foundation, Inc.

NO. 5 (UNTITLED) 1964 oil on canvas 90 x 69"

Collection of Christopher Rothko

UNTITLED (PLUM AND BROWN) 1964 oil on canvas 81 x 69 1/8"

Private collection

NO. 3 1967 oil on canvas 66 ¼ x 68"

Collection of Kate Rothko Prizel

UNTITLED 1968 acrylic on paper mounted on board 33 ½ x 25 ½"

Private collection

Some viewers struggle with the work of the 1960s, suggesting most typically that the generally darker colors are less appealing. I don't believe, however, that this is the primary reason for their difficulty. For what began to change subtly, several years after my father's palette began to darken, was the means he used to express the emotional content of the work. As he stripped away still more layers in search of clarity, the paintings became formally tighter, the rectangles more regular in shape, the layers of color reduced, and brushwork less and less visible until it reappeared again in dramatic fashion in the last two years of his life. This further simplification of his style can give the impression of less energy; of emotional restraint in comparison to the outpourings of feeling in the sensuous and extroverted works of the 1950s.

It is not the case, however, that these works are any less driven by emotion, or less formed from it, than their predecessors. It is simply that the emotional material has become highly focused, and the content more specific. Color still carried the message, looking to engage with our innermost selves, but rather than bright, broad brushstrokes of feeling, we are presented with more pinpointed emotions, expressed through subtle interplay of very carefully juxtaposed colors.

—Christopher Rothko

UNTITLED 1968 acrylic on paper mounted on masonite $39\,^{3}/_{16} \times 24\,^{1}/_{2}$"

Collection of Kate Rothko Prizel

08994

UNTITLED 1968 acrylic on paper mounted on board 32 3/8 x 25"

Collection of Kate Rothko Prizel

The dark colors alone cannot account for the slower tempo of the paintings of this period. The enormous scale of many of these works also plays a significant role. Although there is, as ever, variation, the 1960s works tend to be larger than their counterparts from the 1950s. They simply require more time for us to take them in. And not only do we have more area to scan, Rothko has created a landscape where we may lose ourselves; a painting becomes almost a world of its own, where we find ourselves caught up and lingering beyond our conscious intention to stay.

—Christopher Rothko

UNTITLED 1968 acrylic and ink on paper 58 x 40 3/4"

Collection of Kate Rothko Prizel

UNTITLED 1969 acrylic and ink on paper mounted on canvas 71 13/16 x 42"

Collection of Kate Rothko Prizel

UNTITLED 1969 acrylic and ink on paper 83 ½ x 59 ¾"

Collection of Christopher Rothko

I became a painter because I wanted to raise painting to the level of poignancy of music and poetry.

—Mark Rothko

UNTITLED 1969 acrylic and ink on paper 72 1/16 x 42 1/16"

Collection of Christopher Rothko

UNTITLED 1969 acrylic on paper 51 5/8 x 41"

Collection of Christopher Rothko

32 **NO. 3** 1967

oil on canvas 66 1/4 x 68"
Collection of Kate Rothko Prizel

34 **UNTITLED** 1968

acrylic on paper mounted on board 33 1/2 x 25 1/2"
Private collection

38 **UNTITLED** 1968

acrylic on paper mounted on masonite 39 3/16 x 24 1/2"
Collection of Kate Rothko Prizel

40 **UNTITLED** 1968

acrylic on paper mounted on board 32 3/8 x 25"
Collection of Kate Rothko Prizel

42 **UNTITLED** 1968

acrylic and ink on paper 58 x 40 3/4"
Collection of Kate Rothko Prizel

44 **UNTITLED** 1969

acrylic and ink on paper mounted on canvas 71 13/16 x 42"
Collection of Kate Rothko Prizel

46 **UNTITLED** 1969

acrylic and ink on paper 83 1/2 x 59 3/4"
Collection of Christopher Rothko

48 **UNTITLED** 1969

acrylic and ink on paper 72 1/16 x 42 1/16"
Collection of Christopher Rothko

50 **UNTITLED** 1969

acrylic on paper 51 5/8 x 41"
Collection of Christopher Rothko

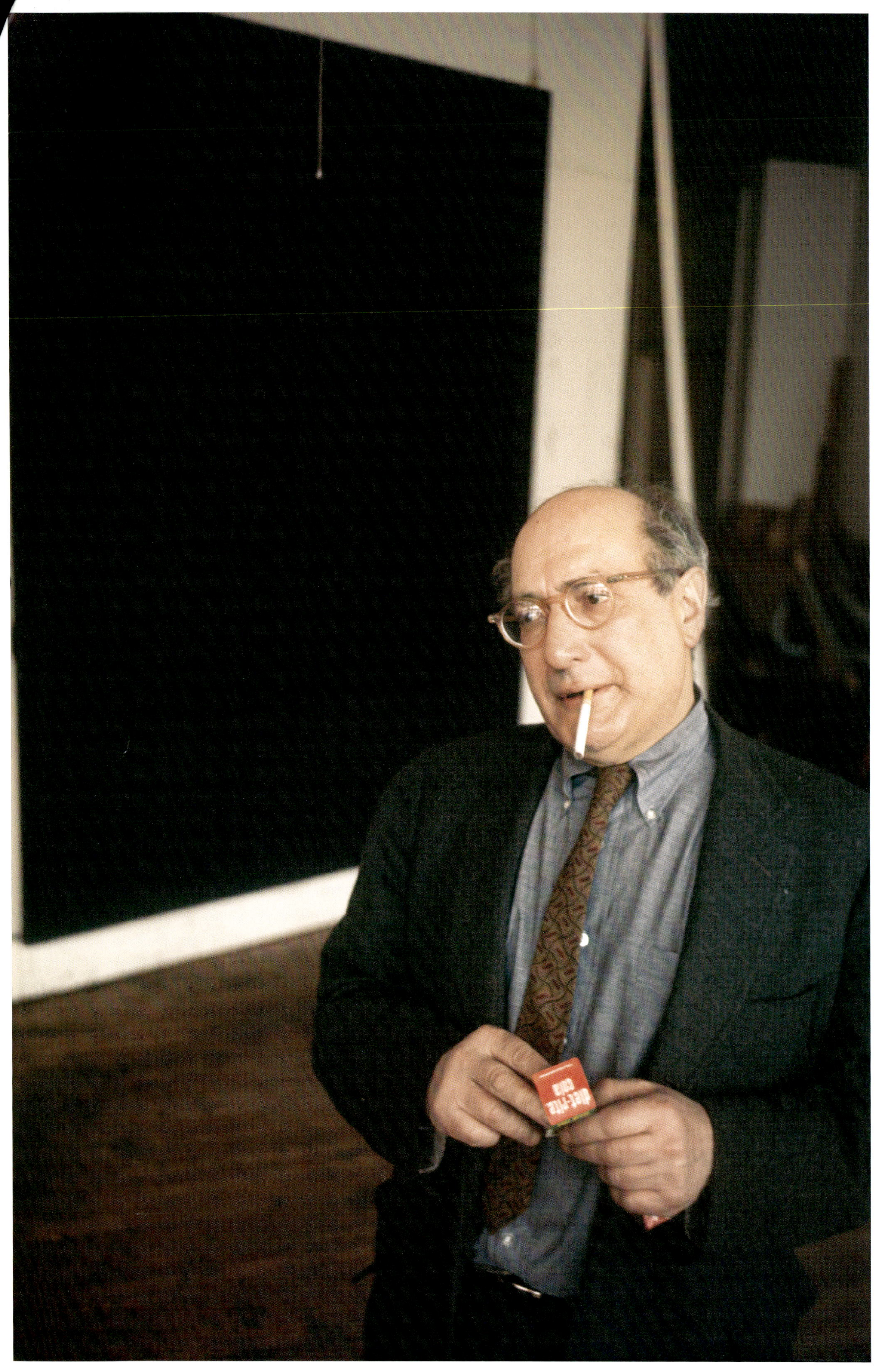

ACKNOWLEDGEMENTS

I have been considering the presentation of Rothko's dark palette paintings for many years. The success in finally bringing this set of paintings together is the product of a group effort. Chief among them are the artist's children, Kate Rothko Prizel and Christopher Rothko, for their suggestions and uncompromising support of this exhibition. In certain instances, they exchanged works from their personal collections with museums to secure our loans.

To the private collectors, you have my gratitude for parting with your treasures and for your sense of responsibility in allowing these extraordinary works to be shared with a greater audience.

To the museum directors and their staff who graciously loaned masterpieces to our presentation, you have our sincere thanks. They include: Janne Sirén, Albright-Knox Art Gallery; Glenn Lowry and Ann Temkin, Museum of Modern Art; Earl A. Powell III and Harry Cooper, National Gallery of Art, Washington D.C.; and Alex Nyerges, Virginia Museum of Fine Arts.

Lastly, my thanks to my assistant, Rachel Boyle, for her constant support, and to Marc Glimcher for his involvement in the selection, his counsel, and encouragement in helping me fulfill this dream exhibition.

A.G.

Cover and endpapers: Mark Rothko, 1485 First Avenue studio, New York, 1964

Page 4: View of East 69th Street, New York. Rothko's studio, 157 East 69th Street, third from left

Page 6–7: Mark Rothko in his studio, New York, NY, c. 1964–1968

Page 8: *Black in Deep Red*, 1958 (detail); 13 (full view)

Page 9: Mark Rothko, "Address to Pratt Institute, November 1958," in *Writings on Art*. (New Haven and London: Yale University Press, 2006), 125–26.

Page 12: Christopher Rothko, "The Quiet Dominance of Form," in *Mark Rothko: From The Inside Out*. (New Haven and London: Yale University Press, 2015), 65.

Page 19: Christopher Rothko, "The Seagram Murals: The Epic and The Myth," in *Mark Rothko: From The Inside Out*. (New Haven and London: Yale University Press, 2015), 139.

Page 26: Mark Rothko quoted in Selden Rodman, in *Conversations with Artists* (New York: Capricorn Books, 1961), 93.

Page 36: *Untitled*, 1968 (detail); 35 (full view)

Page 37: Christopher Rothko, "Mark Rothko and the Inner World," in *Mark Rothko: From The Inside Out*. (New Haven and London: Yale University Press, 2015), 36–37.

Page 42: Christopher Rothko, "The Mastery of the '60s," In *Mark Rothko: From The Inside Out*. (New Haven and London: Yale University Press, 2015), 203.

Page 48: Mark Rothko quoted in Brian O'Doherty, in *The Voice and Myth of American Masters* (New York: Random House, 1973), 153.

Pages 52–53: *Untitled*, 1969 (detail); 51 (full view)

Photography:
Courtesy Albright-Knox Art Gallery; p. 23
Tom Barratt; pp. 47–53
Dan Budnik, © Dan Budnik, all rights reserved; cover, endpapers, p. 56
Christopher Burke Studio; pp. 11, 29, 33, 39
Edmund Vincent Gillon / Museum of the City of New York; p. 4
Alexander Liberman, courtesy The Getty Research Institute, © J. Paul Getty Trust; pp. 6–7
Kerry Ryan McFate; pp. 41–43
The Museum of Modern Art, © The Museum of Modern Art / Licensed by SCALA / Art Resource, NY; p. 15
Courtesy National Gallery of Art, Washington; p. 27
Hickey Robertson; p. 25
Courtesy The Mark Rothko Foundation; pp. 16–18
Courtesy Sotheby's; p. 31
Katherine Wetzel, © Virginia Museum of Fine Arts; p. 21
Ellen Page Wilson; pp. 35, 36, 45

Design: Tomo Makiura and Mine Suda

Production: Pace Gallery

Color Correction: Motohiko Tokuta

Printing: Meridian Printing, East Greenwich, Rhode Island

Library of Congress Control Number: 2016954614

ISBN: 978-1-935410-87-4

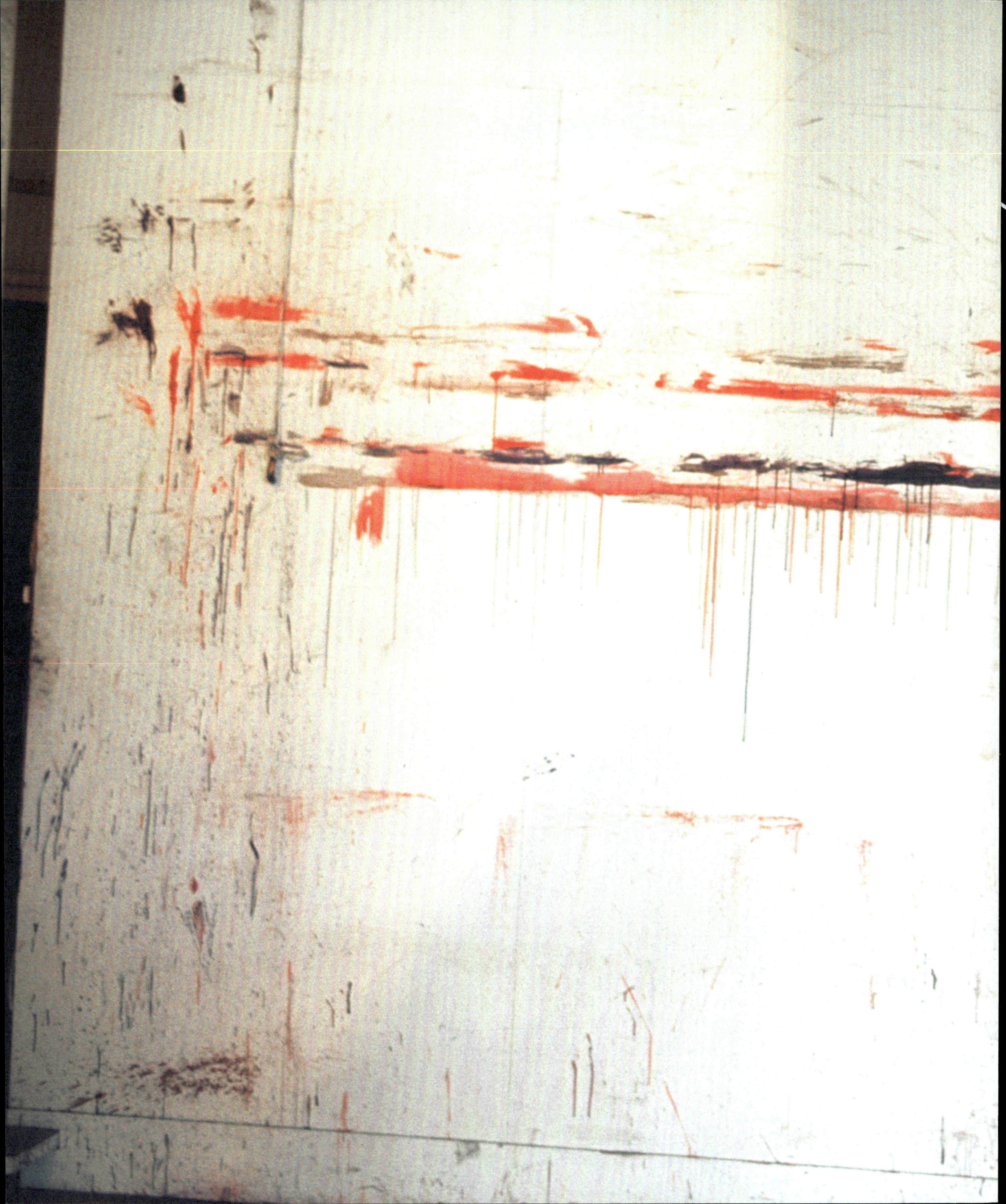